NEOLOGIC THOUGHT
****

AH'KHEMU

Copyright © 2017 Ricky Gaines

All rights reserved. This book or any portion thereof may not be reproduced or used in any manner whatsoever without the express written permission of the publisher except for the use of brief quotations in a book review or scholarly journal.

This is a book of poetry. Any references or similarities to actual events, real people, living or dead, or to real locales are intended to give the book of poetry a sense of reality. Any similarity in other names, characters, places, and incidents is entirely coincidental.

First Printing: 2017

ISBN- 978-1-7324049-2-2

Published by Ricky Gaines

Cover Design: F. Ruiz

Senior Editor: A. Parra

Assistant Editor: Ricky Gaines

Capital Gaines LLC
4023 Kennett Pike #2082
Wilmington DE 19807
Email: cp@capitalgaines.com
Website: www.capgainesllc.com
Phone: 302-433-6777

Dedication

This novel is dedicated to big dreamers, to real hustlers, and to the usefulness of transferable skills...

To our Capital Gaines LLC team - Thank you for having the courage, faith, and confidence to stick with me on this legitimate, creative mission.

To the author -
Congratulations!

Cheers to longevity, healthy living, and even bigger dreams.
To our friends, family, supporters, and readers from every culture - all over the world, THANK YOU, THANK YOU, THANK YOU.

Enjoy the novel, and please, spread the word.

Ricky Gaines / Slick-G / Publisher

NEOLOGIC THOUGHT
****
AH'KHEMU

TABLE OF CONTENTS

1. Black Male Urban Life...1-20

2. Black Feminine Greatness...21-37

3. Black Social Thought...38-54

4. Critiques on Black Culture...55-73

5. Black Intellectual Poems...71-87

6. Bonus Poem: Rimz',Timz', and Gemz'...88

-NOTE-

*Ah'Khemu — means — "He who lives in the abode of the creator and chronicles the heavenly cosmos of creation".

NEOLOGIC THOUGHT

1) YOUR Fast Lane Has One Exit

VOOOM VOOM -

I'll race you to your doom —

you'll find it right next to your tomb

your trophy is death —

because of all that reckless driving through life's open course

has now left you gasping for breath

Due to this failed economic pursuit of illegal prosperity —

those Gullewing doors on your Mercedes has opened you up for visual transparency —

all that changing lanes —

have complicated a few thangs —

I bet you wish it wasn't too late to trade in that devilish sports car for a brand new Land Rover or a

Range —

But, this highway was made for your kind —

ever since "street racing" school, trouble for you was never hard to find —

so now it's time for you to stand at the podium —

AH'KHEMU

NEOLOGIC THOUGHT

at the winner's circle so you can receive what's tantamount to a deadly champagne dowse of sodium.

2) Baller Street Rule's

I'ma Wolf-Spider,

The webs I cast on these street's leaves sucka's dangling for being fake ass riders —

My click's financial net's are cast wider —

the math is simple niggah, I'ma the divider-

so refrain from playin bitch-boy games fo' you fuck around and run into a collider—

In my section, I'm the main provider.

When it comes to material wealth I'ma real chick magnet, yeah I'ma subscriber

As my "Hood's" uniter, my main concern is turf politics that causes miasmata

On this trail... Violence, envy and faulty cops campaign under the cloak of deadly veils...

That's made you a persona non grata - A pariah in these streets, fabricated with a stigmata-

When you acquire wealth, power and prestige they're only commendable-

when you have a loyal and knowledgeable coterie, who also view betrayal of it's brethren as being condemnable-To Death!

NEOLOGIC THOUGHT

3) Fake Flossin

These fraudulent ass status seekers

will, lie, steal and kill in order to climb up the urban social ladder,

and they don't care if their wearing high-hill pumps or exotic sneakers —

The weal of the young whether strong or weaker —

are all eagerly craving for the "bravura" lime-light which mimics the earth's power out-put of ether .

High siders of this sort are convinced that regular chicken is equivalent to being foie gras —

even their desire to live in opulence, real or fake extravagance

isn't frowned upon nor looked as a faux

just ask any trill nigga —

Certainly the'll say it's enough to give a person pause.

Muthafucka's wearing gaudy amounts of 'Bort Stone' speckled jewelry —

make's for good conversational fodder as a celebrated variety of buffoonery —

So why should we bother with people out of tune with their Chi-

living above their means-trying to keep up with 'BIG KAHUNAS' of the sea

And they wonder why all this fakism leads to hate mixed with envy.

NEOLOGIC THOUGHT

<u>4) Hustle's Haven</u>

The inner-city landscape, is actually a thriving bazar —

where hot good's, hot flesh and hot shots push, hock and solicit everything that's illicit

from exotic-toxic bootys to custom cars —

No other conurbation can offer these cheap creature-comforts or amenities

It's a criminals' oasis by far.

The trap house, the gambling shack and the whore house will provide liaisons

on many occasions —

because it's to stroke the hustler's ambition by pussy persuasion

except when 5-0 is part of the equation.

The reality is, 'Instant Gratification'

has swept up our youth's vivid imagination

with fraudulent 'hood schemes' of social aspirations —

And a street perceived notion-

that's mutated into a dystopian believed devotion —

For these urban entrepreneurs,

education and hard work are no longer viable paths to prosperity

shinny bort stones and dreck clothing have become a part of their hood ethics

and their posterity.

America's version of 'favelas' birth both millionaires —

and beautiful chick's with intoxicating luscious derrieres

it's hood etiquette we've deemed to be 'savoir faire'

The ghetto's are social black holes —

there will always be street profiteers,

privateers and puppeteers

who will take whatever they think is theirs.

It's the hood life and in America everybody owes.

NEOLOGIC THOUGHT

5) The Block Is Where My Heart's At!

The only allegiance I have

is to my street corner —

My occupation breeds contempt...

because I lack any-kind of moral code

I'ma street Performa'

I'm hood certified so I'm exempt...

My night's are long —

cause my hustle game is strong —

please don't get me wrong — I love my folks but, I'm on my own.

I'm not built for some 9 to 5

No-way in hell —

Shit, I keep 5 for 9 with what I sell.

I'm trying to eat on these streets

Are we clear?

I'ma push what's popping in the hood's atmosphere —

and if I have to instill a little fear—

I will...

So these nigga's know I'm for real.

I don't have any ambivalence

I never struggle with it —

I push narcotics so magnificent

I'd smuggle drug's across the boarder

Just to get it —

and oh' boy, this is the type of shit that has the FEDS quite livid —

So check my swag, it's an open exhibit —

I love 'green' like Kermit the fog

~I'MA GO GET IT...

RIBBIT!~

RIBBIT!~

6) Got Dope

If you have dope,

It can reward you with a little wealth —

If you've got dope,

It can also be very harmful to your health

If you got dope,

It all depends on what kind —

If you got dope,

there will always be a market to provide —

If you got dope,

your lively hood could be well defined —

If you got dope,

using it should never cross your mind —

If you got dope,

death or prison is a real possibility in due time —

If you got dope,

every low-life scoundrel will purport to being a friend —

And because you have this dope,

their true intentions won't be revealed until the bitter end —

but by then,

It'll be too late, because —you've got dope.

NEOLOGIC THOUGHT

7) Misplaced Devotions

The belief in things that are immaterial, has captivated our youth's wonderment-

this materialized worship has fed their sexual inclinations, uncontrollable drug

dependence, and self obsessed image enslavement.

These identifying markers

are indicators to their socio-pathos —

It's what they equate with being their relevant ethos —

Having their emotions exposed and on display is in contrast with their inflated egos —

As the story goes —

We reap what we sow...

As black males, we're so critical

in our charge over social mistreatment —

yet, we've failed to recognize our own self de-basement —

We're the only race of men that considers

a slanderous word like 'nigga'

as a term of endearment —

What do you expect after four centuries of anti-social experiments —
What blooms are mentally foul-smelling Human Spirits
Which becomes this long lasting cultural impairment.

8) Thug Neurosis

This mental plague can't be quantified,

now, I'm no social theorist —

However, I do know that we're in desperate need of a cultural purist.—

I have no qualms with my urban 'borne' derelictions-

I was birthed from "AMERICA'S" toxic soil

and didn't receive alms from those pious folks

sworn to benevolent predilections.

Maybe this explains, why me and my like-kind

commits crimes

such as, drug dealing', pimping', and stealing'.

which then turns to raping', robbing' and killing'.

As though we're perverted benisons —

when in reality, me and my like-kind are sociopathic and psychologically malicious.

We scream 'THUG LIFE', because of our antinomic position -

being a disenfranchised black male,

on a large scale,

this gives reason for our forensic criminal disposition —

which wasn't of its own volition —

this cunning socio-epithet,

might as well be an epitaph

for an inner-city youth deemed emotionally inert decomposition.

NEOLOGIC THOUGHT

9) What's the meaning of being 'TRILL

For those un-familiar with Ebonic vernacular

It means keepin' it true and real —

an amalgamated word people have trouble

tryin' to feel-

I guess being fake, plastic and a fraud,

has become socially applauded and openly

lauded so why conceal?-

Envy, and betrayal

are as accepted as, hates portrayal,

so why not do it with zeal.

Still it's easy and it doesn't require you to have much skill —

only the will,

especially since fame is rewarded off of meretricious appeal —

and these crazy ass people are for real

to them, it's honorable to lie, cheat and steal —

hell, in some case's even rob, beat and kill.

How do you contend with an apathetic

segment that's unnerving within its own bathetic spiel —

only in it for life's trivial frills —

So beware of their emotive feelings,

their never random,

it's a havoc done in tandem,

and it's what greases their ego's wheel.

NEOLOGIC THOUGHT

10) Black-Male Vulgarism

There are some really obnoxious niggah's

amongst my kind —

who can't seem to comprehend what being

noxious can trigger as if their blind —

There's nothing innocuous about celebrating

whose corner spot is bigger —

or who has the most violent hitters —

these obstreperous niggah's,

have formed an unorganized malefic order

of thoughtless killers.

This warped hood meticulousness,

has replaced our once promising young

leaders —

with new age problem feeders.

Astonishingly enough, Ghetto decadence reigns,

because of their tireless pursuit

of luxuriant exotics-like flashy cars, fancy clothes

and blinged out gem-stones,

It's braggadocio hood ergonomics —

no, it's more like being a serial caricature

of buffoonery

otherwise called a quixotic —

These self-depreciating beings

are being reduced into irrelevant neurotics —

while some are chronically addicted

to the false temperance of narcotics —

never once pondering the lure,

of an "Insistent" gratifying cure

from the subtropics.

The sheer brevity of this life style —

contradicts the essence of longevity,

which makes living life worthwhile —

their levity has vanished now —

because these inner-city gamin's

have pledged their allegiance to allegoric acts

NEOLOGIC THOUGHT

run afoul.

11) Her Reflective Presence

On a hot summer's day-

as I cast this sweeping glance across the bay —

something visceral within me starts my thoughts to say:

What is it I see —

that shimmers over the sea.

It sparkles and glistens —

as if its beckoning me to listen —

to the soothing sound wave that it conveys

what Her reflection would be if it wasn't missing.

My internal telemetry —

has vocalized Her external imagery —

allowing Her reflection to be cast right before me —

all the while, She's been standing right beside me the whole time.

And I never noticed Her presence,

because the ocean's ability to transfix held my gaze —

which felt more like I was in a daze —

so now I'm me re-viewing Her perfection.

12) Her Ancient Future-Black Femininity

Our nubile Queens have no equals

amongst their gender—

their known the world over

because of their beatific splendor —

They've always radiated

and accentuated a style

that's vaguely familiar to our time —

its reminiscent of a time, and

quite similar to what's called divine —

when our Nubian Queens feared no contenders, and vanquished all other pretenders.

Their place in the annuals of history is replete —

which evince mankind prostrated at the mother's immortal feet-

Humanities God-mother is so sensual and complete

She's equipped with love and compassion that's so sweet,

it's more durable than any steel or concrete.

This human oasis to the African race -

in which no mortal can ever replace

AH'KHEMU

A beautiful black sentient more vast than outer space —

Who was present when creation took place —

now watches Her off-spring defile, debase and deface -

our planet, that's consumed in toxic waste —

these foul parasites need to be removed with haste -

so the rest of Her children can be renewed in her essence that's full of grace.

NEOLOGIC THOUGHT

13) The Black Woman's Will to Persevere

Whether on the late-night streets,

walking to attract prospective "John's" to treat,

or if it's as a domestic-made to clean floors —

She'll endure bouts of public and self-degrading insults to feed her family and more.

There isn't a sacrifice she won't make,

to ensure of her family's continuity —

She will dutifully assume both parental roles,

to give her children a firm sense of security —

and her unconditional love comes with no cost,

because she seeks no gratuity.

Her ability to navigate through-out life's ever changing landscape speaks of determination -

She's possessed with the foresight to interpret complex issues,

which explains her keen and clear social observations.

The essence of this true super-woman, is black and non-fiction —

She will genuflect to one, in order to gain any favorable positions.

Her love's compassion is unparalleled

She's quick to step in to correct the wrongs where everyone else has failed.

To her it doesn't matter the conflict,

or how severe —

no matter what, these black women know how to persevere.

NEOLOGIC THOUGHT

14) A'niyah's Rhapsody

The vivacity I express,

from seeing my beautiful girl's smile —

replaces the vitriol,

I once held for life that was never worthwhile —

Your presence is always in distance,

no matter the miles —

Your magnificence is reminiscent

of the Ancient Straight's of the Khemetic blue and white Nile's.

A precious gift given to me from infinity —

an exquisite creature,

that completes her parents' trinity.

You were birth from 'amorous' disposition —

a subtle creature,

with 'ebony-aesthetic features'

concludes a prodigious composition —

and it's going to take 'mirth' —

which can heal the soul,

but, how do you become ready to accept such a life changing proposition.

Putting her traits aside —

I'm more concerned with our interwoven personalities,

hoping they don't collide —

being that we're both Gemini's,

with complex entities that reside —

deep down inside —

and maybe this loving father's pure unconditional love,

can assist with any emotional divides —

that life's reoccurring dramatic themes are sure to provide...

NEOLOGIC THOUGHT

15) She's God's Creation

I take this heart,

which beats of pure love —

and carefully place it in your chest,

where it fits as snug as a surgeon's glove.

Once I begin to close her incision —

I gently move about,

ensuring it's done with precision.

These delicately trained hands,

hold one of nature's "Original" beauties —

the passion in which I possess,

to design this Goddess,

is in contrast with creations duties.

I'm not some mad scientist and this isn't an illusion —

the perfect female creature mankind has ever seen will be their ultimate conclusion.

With true competence and dare —

complete with plenty of time to spare,

a process that's meant to speed up conversion

NEOLOGIC THOUGHT

so once she's awakened,

it will allow for easy acceptance and immersion.

What Dr. Frankenstein created, was deemed a monster...

what I've created, is an enlightened soul

that glow's

and has no mortal master.

16) Constant Reverence

To praise you is only half a treat —

To be near you is only half complete —

there is no in-between,

when it concerns you and who you are,

I am intoxicated by your mystique —

I get severe chills up my spin,

whenever I hear you speak.

The sound of your voice,

is soothing to my soul,

even from the words that you utter—

trying to describe you only make's me stutter,

due to the divine feeling in which you humbly bestow.

There isn't enough words in the English lexicon,

to equate one aspect of who or what you are —

there aren't enough 'superlatives' to find,

because your other-worldly and you might as well be from the planet mars.

NEOLOGIC THOUGHT

Not even Earth's highest peaks,

its deepest sea's nor its longest stretch of land —

these are enormous measures that make you —

the black woman —

truly incomparable to man.

17) A Friendship Born from Love

Every time I think about you, my mind turns to remembrance

the opportunity to experience life's joy with you rectifies my ambivalence.

I can recall every year of our inception.

Especially, the times where the hardships wouldn't seem to let up —

Right down to me sittin' here reminiscing about how enthusiastic you were about us not giving up.

I never thought love would find me in the form of you -

Maybe life really does have this unique way of revealing something old - is actually new.

I wish I'd paid more attention to us from the start —

I could've made a concerted effort to play my God-given part —

Whoever said friend's could never be lovers obviously didn't know the truth,

Human nature won't allow you to handcuff the heart —

Forsaking those who are good to you,

for what feels good to you can't be viewed as being a move that's smart.

18) Never Once

Never once has there been a time where you've turned your back on me.

Even when I didn't respect you or me, you were there.

Never Once — Did you let me struggle without offering your help,

even though I found myself in all sort's of trouble,

you always held out hope for me.

Never Once — Has time gone by without you not showing real concern for my well-being,

even when I didn't care about myself, you did.

Never Once Would you let an argument we had linger on without first reaching out and

being the first to forgive,

even though I was the one to blame,

It didn't matter to you... NEVER ONCE!!!

NEOLOGIC THOUGHT

19) Sweet and Tangy

Sour apples, sour plums —

sweet nectarine are as tasty as her cum.

It's nature's in-toxicating nectar —

that's carried through the female vectors.

That forbidden root —

nestled under her pleasure cove,

was found while trolling through her paradise.

Open for bidding —

your fruit —

wrestled to plunder her treasure trove.

'some sound advice',

you'd rather play Russian roulette,

than rolling these pair of dice.

Once you get a whiff of her entrancing aroma —

Her sweet succulent syrup will put that ass in a coma.

They say,

It's Mother Nature's way

Of producing creations version of an aphrodisiac —

But, I've come to construe this as an acidulous serum,

that has turned most of today's men into perverted-sexual-maniacs.

NEOLOGIC THOUGHT

20) Can You Hear Their Cry

These young nubile aged mothers are continuously stressed-

caring for fatherless children the only way they know best-

their precious face's s reveal tired expressions in desperate need of rest-

especially, from a judgmental society that's unrelenting in it's quest,

to demoralize and vilify them, once they've failed love's test.

How can they help themselves, in order to put back together all the scattered pieces -

It's quite daunting when their stuck in a social system plagued with malfeasance.

With little hope or support, their left with unanswered prayers-

given their temperance is low, because of their haphazard love affair's-which has released a bevy of unrequited emotionless flair.

These ill-fated dreams are part of their reality-

dysfunctional relationships that have no finality-

this ever extended causality becomes seriously devoid of clear rationality-

and it's left these inner-city beings, one more voiceless character of banality.

21) A Simplistic Affair

It has always been easy to love you-

your adoring nature,

makes it fun to explore you-

my emotions remain even keeled whenever I'm around you-

love's compassion,

life's inspiration and strength complements you-

For me, I have but one task, and that is to cherish, honor and protect you-

these are the requirements needed to secure you-

but, most importantly, respect you.

22) In Love's Rearview

It's been said, "If you love someone long enough, you should be willing to let them go",

I say, "rubbish"!

When your love's real-

It can with-stand or resist any and all attempts to steal-

Unless that true passion your love hasn't had a chance to reveal.

Once the euphoria has come and passed,

your heart starts to realize the emotional highs fail to last.

Now your empathy wonder's-

If this is the person you care so deeply about,

thoughts ponder-

The amorous feelings and emotional depth,

of those who've failed and are the first responders.

Trying to corner love is pretty much the luck of the draw-

If you happen to find it, secure it as if it's a baby joy in it's mother's maw.

Now if this happens to you,

Remember, "your always in love's rear-view"!

23) Intellectual Hoodlums

The University of the streets-

whose student body, is comprised of hustla's, whore's and cheats-

Who dwell in an unruly urban area,

where its scholar athletes dictate who play's and who competes-

you must be capitalistically cunning if you plan to eat-

For every person addicted to these treacherous and unscrupulous streets-

their ambivalence postpones the illicit treasures they seek.

The Graduate students or O.G.'s of this world narrates for the youth,

all the pleasures to be reaped-

what's easily procured and laid at your feet-

'POP-QUIZZ'...

What's all substance and has no meat?-

Explicit advertisement with offers that entice street scholars to make claims they say can't be beat-

But, just as long as your discrete-

becoming a student of manipulation can have some value to people you happen to meet-

NEOLOGIC THOUGHT

Remember, It's no surrender or retreat-

You must however, practice due diligence with your entrepreneurial endeavors,

before the games complete-

either way, It's success or death before you accept a defeat-

So, let this be a true testament to all discerning hoodlums-

acquire knowledge, wisdom and discipline before power

If not, look at the perils of the those who've caused mayhem and pandemonium.

Yes, the ones who've failed, and who are sitting within the overcrowding prisons.

Young Brother & Sister...

Get an education and live free through your intellectual abilities...

24) Birth of a Hoodlum

On 5-24-81, at the tender age of seven, my life in criminality had begun-

It all started with the clever pilferage of my cousin's gun-

this curiosity

as a wondering black youth,

would eventually turn into my virtuosity,

that would lead me on this sustained prison run-

and this is when those unforgiving streets, with a menagerie of young ruffians

would indoctrinate a naive 12-year-old into a life time of crime labeled as being fun-

During this phase of my life there weren't any warnings to heed-

I was this fast growing steed-

with no rein's in place to halt what these wicked streets would breed-

with alarming speed, and it's all very true indeed.

My ever increasing exploits over the years would cost me many relationships

and my freedom countless times-

All for the lore of urban riches,

NEOLOGIC THOUGHT

which spoke to an unstrung inner urge that was infatuated with crime-

my fuzzy thinking at that time 'Why chase a slow nickel - when you can catch a fast dime'-

now this skewed logic has me in prison for life while in my prime-

and Its clearly revealed to me, the true cost of a wasted mind.

Again... Young Brother & Sister...

Get an education and live free through your intellectual abilities...

25) We Were First

Before this world was born from a thirst-

Before the creator decided who should rule this earth-

We were first...

Before mankind began to migrate and disperse-

Before the people became lustful and perverse

We were first...

To fashion civilized culture for the masses-

Constructing monuments-

to universally reveal a rich and glorious past.

While refining the different ethnic classes-

We were first...

To chart the stars of our universe-

While neoteric man-

conceives of some cosmic curse-

To explain what it can't comprehend as to why or what God created first-

Was it from an instant burst-

Was it the dark race-

NEOLOGIC THOUGHT

formed and fashioned from dirt

Was it the planets or the galaxies created in spurts

No, it was you and I...

Humanity, we were first.

26) Black Tainted D.N.A.

The black male segment in this country has historically been the actual subjects of various social and clinical experiments-

From the colonial periods of America, to the 20th century trails in eugenics,

to the syphilitic out-breaks of the Tuskegee experiments-

to now what's become, crack cocaine's lasting will and testament.

These immoral acts-

led to the discovery of more sinister and diabolical facts-

like genetic-genome type warfare devoted to all things Black-

and hoping once complete,

theres enough "Negro" biologically left in-tact.

Because of this amoral predisposition-

The Black man was forced into a position-

to be experimental acquisitions-

that's needed to be debased and studied for the sole supposition-

of some "sick scientist" in need of exact samples,

in order to complete his in-humane medical compositions-

under these kinds of conditions-

NEOLOGIC THOUGHT

It's no wonder the black male suffers from various psycho-neurotic afflictions.

No other race of men-

has ever had to endure these types of unpardonable sins.

Where this composed genetic contamination

has morphed and mutated into this generation of social condemnation.

We are this undesirable element-

that's out-lived what's considered relevant-

yet, we're still this nominally infatuated anomaly-

that's been reduced into a non-entity quite phenomenally.

Society has criminalized us, and some view the Black man as living waste receptacles-

When in reality, we're more akin to being antinomic - thugs, out-laws, gangsta' spectacles-

regardless of what's transpired against the Black man,

America continues to view their hate as being socially acceptable-

and without cohesive dialogue this will continue to plague race relations,

and that is truly regrettable.

27) The Price for Freedom

What are you willing to do to escape life's struggle?-

Would you rob, steal or kill, or would you carry these drugs to smuggle?

Most people aren't faced with these kind of choices -

and when your thought's become plagued by so many voices-

it becomes paramount to drown out all those irrepressible noises-

with the probability of success somehow cloistering the human invoices.

In this land of milk and honey, and alleged freedom-

you're truly not free.

Not even you're alter idem... the second self!

There's always this huge price to pay in order to live here-

whether it's on the tough inner-city streets-

or having coitus under Egyptian cotton sheets-

Your seriously delusive if you thought you could live in this country free and clear-

In America, there's always this astronomical cost for freedom... "Didn't you hear"!

NEOLOGIC THOUGHT

28) The Miscegenation

What was once considered to be taboo-
that it was compared to Zebra stripes from a zoo-
Is now openly lauded in an attempt to pursue-
a course of human gumbo mixed into a creation stew.
Quite frankly,
this isn't out of histories purview-
nothing under the sun is rare or brand new-
The procreation process between various cultures,
is similar to that first taste of exotic fondue,
or this failed ideological curtain of bamboo.
Mankind's miscalculated precepts,
has distorted love's ambiguous virtue-
no matter their pigmentation or hue-
shit,
not even superstitious Ethnic beliers like voodoo
can restrain or contain race mixing from becoming the two.
The my-stories in our genetic link provides neoteric

NEOLOGIC THOUGHT

science with a plethora of clues-

that our unhealthy racial pre-occupation obscures

what's important and continues to confound our social views.

How pathetic,

yet it is so true!

29) Devitalizing Our Blackness

This ambivalence toward creation's black progeny

has to be a part of some hidden agenda-

We're the most venerated,

socially replicated and musically emulated hue,

that's equally imbued with all sorts of colorful stigmas-

we're apart of energies dark essence

with or without its bold evanescence,

which siphons the elucidation aimed at this illumanistic enigma-

and its apparent a heinous malediction,

concocted to cause ebullient confliction,

has become America's favored thematic cinema.

This malison perpetuated towards nature's first sapient,

portends we were created as galactic slaves

tasked with "Electrum (gold) extraction"

by unknown illegal aliens.

Since modern man can't decipher creations iridescent apparatus-

NEOLOGIC THOUGHT

Anglophilic historicity continues to devalue black's natural magnetic status...

The Ancient's ascribe the onyx Race to that of Elysium-

The future will proscribe the rest of mankind,

from the Lord's emporium.

NEOLOGIC THOUGHT

30) POVERTY PIMPIN

"Heyyy Baaaby, you wanna' ride in my Cadillac-

yeah lilt mamma, get in and kick back-

let Big Daddy black show ya whose the Mack"-

This shit is a shame-

these parasitic "imp's" can't refrain,

from exploiting our precious female blessings,

for financial gain-

40 years of this glorified ghetto fame-

has our young black male's celebrating these perverted pitchmen,
who openly prey upon females as if their some form of exotic game.

They tell these naive girls lies, make false promises and offer 'street sage' advice, because it's a trick of the trade-

how else can you convince them to offer up themselves too be laid-

they don't give a damn about their "cohort's" feelings,

just as long as they get paid.

A pimp's axiom is simple: "rain, sleet or snow-

bitch betta' have my money and she already know,

not to come short with my muthafuckin' dough"!

This is "gender extortion" at its best.

Whether it's done freely or forcible, all due's must be met- otherwise those cold and bitter streets is where they'll fret- with real heart-break and regret.

NEOLOGIC THOUGHT

31) P.I.M.P.

(Providing Impulsive Men Pussy)

There's this foul eponym attached to me that's pretty misleading-

upon further review,

you could say out right deceiving-

People like me are often given "rakish" connotations-

with no regards to the adverse inclinations.

When you consult with me,

it's never impromptu-

on rare occasions, I'll arrange a quaint dinner for two.

My business acuity-

doesn't allow for any personal insecurities-

with all my affairs, I like to manage a strong level of professional promiscuity-

So my clients and I can be-aware of any ambiguities-

no I.O.U(s) or payment's in perpetuity.

In this "sphere" of instant gratification-

I must remain ever vigilant of the law,

and all of its ramifications-

NEOLOGIC THOUGHT

because how I operate,

there's no need for unwanted public agitation-

Most purveyors don't embody the social sophistication-

that's needed,

to navigate a "sybaritic" landscape and deal with wealth's perversities in all its manifestations.

See, In this life,

you're never promised wealth, power nor prestige-

but when you vie for my services,

I'll procure the finest exotics your five- senses have ever laid siege.

32) The Black Essence

This shroud of mystery accentuates our attraction-

Its dark unknown and alluring undertones,

won't allow for mere interactions.

This innate ability to transpose its perception-

began in utero-the womb,

that was caused through creation's boom.

Which will always be viewed through the glaring tints of conception...

with a slight tinge of perfection.

The way Black has been vilified, and subsequently deified shows this contradiction is the enigma-

and when you're seen as an innominate, who continuously innovates cultural social trends for others to emulate and somehow we're still placed with negative stigmas.

This chaotic cultural order never explains why nature is perceived as being negative-

and life is considered the quintessential positive-

"what the hell gives"?

Take these 3 stimulants for instance-

NEOLOGIC THOUGHT

oil, soil and coffee beans on high boil,

their stimuli matters, as anti-matter is to dark matter, there in-lays our significance.

AH'KHEMU

33) These Street's Speak for No One

The glorification of the black ghetto existence-

is this driving force,

why urban degradation proceeds with persistence-

Inner-city profiteers bleed the blocks of the destitute without fear of resistance.

This reverse ameliorative acculturation-

helped to mentally displaced these urbanites in need of true cultural restoration.

The will in all of us speaks to an unyielding fortitude,

as we're forced to thrive around decadence and ruin- they've made hustlin' into a crime,

claim gentrifying the poor is only a matter of time

this shit ain't sublime

nor am I blind

I'm not anti-Semitic, but this is what's referred to as jewin'

No one seems to care about our voice or how we're doin'

whether we're complaining about the toxic waste,

or talking about our youth who are noxious with haste,

NEOLOGIC THOUGHT

there isn't a monkey to get off our backs,

It's more like a "got damn" bruin,

and this is the only truth worth spewin'.

34) To Tell A Truth

When you touch upon the subject of enlightenment and its practical application towards everyday life.

It becomes a paramount topic that needs to be addressed, and understood quite intellectually.

It's not about what we think we know,

It's about how we use what we know.

Just because we may possess a vast vocabulary and articulate it well,

doesn't make a person enlightened.

Someone who speaks often, freely and uncensored,

is sometimes frowned upon. Not because he or she expresses their thought's, but because they don't know when to shut the fuck up!

Talking doesn't draw any tangible conclusions other than exhibiting a transparent facade.

There's a huge difference between talking about something happening or making something happen.

Nothing in this life is given freely other than the precious air we breathe.

Especially, anything of real substance.

A valued commodity is respect and It's priceless.

NEOLOGIC THOUGHT

Most of the time, what's taking place on the surface, is quite different from what's transpiring below it.

Knowing the world we live in everyone is not privy to what he or she knows.

What Organization would want associates who couldn't suppress their tongue.

The reason why elites are in perpetual power, is because they understand the fallacy of the emotive tongue,

and once you know how to implicature relevant-bit-information, that's when it becomes a means to an end.

35) Our Ebony Mask

The real beauty of the African people

can't be found in their unique features-

nor can it be found in any of nature's other creatures-

This was an arcane gift,

bestowed on humanities first teachers.

There isn't a hue that comes close to black's pronounced magnitude-

Even the origins of light

was birth from this exactitude-

It's why pigmentation caste wars over the centuries would ultimately decide who would rule the multitudes-

existence's dark essence permeates in such infinitude.

Our true talent is in our creative power of innovation-

we're characteristically an urbane people,

who happen to be architecturally arcane with no equals,

whose now last in a society that's too reliant on any technologic illumination-

In order to recapture our aesthetics as the first race, We need an identity restoration... "First"!

NEOLOGIC THOUGHT

One things for certain-

when you want to see the "finest swag" in pop culture,

just pull back-black-society's curtain.

We're possessed with an overwhelming persona

that's naturally portrayed-

but, we've allowed far too many-"others"-into an aura in which they've betrayed,

we're like this human canvas, which life paints in cascades.

What an artistic task-

trying to capture my ebony mask.

36) It's Not About The Sex

I continually fight back my urge to explore you-

when I can't completely contain my impulsive surges,

I intentionally try to ignore you-

so baby, I implore you,

please understand my predicament or should I say,

restrict the dick is meant but I assure you-

that I completely adore you.

You're exactly my type-

I'm not making any excuses, I just want to make sure everything's right-

I'm not trying to give you my penile gland,

I'm trying to get in your pineal gland for tonight-

YEAH, that's right-

no sex is the game,

love-making to your mind is my aim.

NEOLOGIC THOUGHT

37) I Was Once Her Husband

There was a time,

when this beautiful woman named Alicia,

cherished my affections-

There was also a time where I was estranged and failed to provide any financial protection

Even during my times spent in jail-

she transmitted unconditional love and support,

that epitomizes the essence of espousal hail-

A beautiful wife complete, yet so frail-

but, when I'd come home,

all she'd receive from me is heart ache and betrayal.

For over 19 years I've been a burden whose been undeserving of her support I've received yet perverted.

The only thing left for me is a daughter

who inspires self-respect-

it's a second chance for me to get it right,

and she deserves nothing less-

than a committed father capable of doing his absolute best.

I once thought of asking her for her forgiveness-

but the last few years have shown me our marital history isn't something that needs to be revisited-

and her animus feelings I don't want to witness.

I was once a significant other-

now I'm a divorcee,

and she's a single mother-

whether she knows it or not,

I've never stopped loving her.

NEOLOGIC THOUGHT

38) My Heart Also Bleeds

I've taken to heart the travails of an oppressed people-Knowing from personal experience what It's like to be reviled and vilipend as an unequal-

This element of hate is our reoccurring sequel

I have very strong feelings

that are repressed forms of compassion-

I want to open my heart's emotive and restorative power in unpretentious fashion-

This unleashed passion-

left to its own devices,

becomes unbridled love that's not govern by ration.

The crimson elixir that course's through your body-

originates from a pumping station every soul has,

some pure and some shoddy-

Having the chords to your heart constantly pulled,

shouldn't be expected as an accepted past time or casual hobby.

39) This Amative Abyss

I've given away my love's desire freely and its done without exception-

nor with any fear of rejection

Emotive love under expressed,

won't diminish my capacity to further open up myself

for inspection-

we all experience moments of internal dejection-

but I refuse to go thru life bitterly lamenting over love's imperfections.

I opened myself up, so people could explore my compassions depth-

The emotions one possess can be vast,

and also gasp for equal breathe.

When you freely dive in loves ocean.

The swimmer must abide by the laws of the sea-

being perceptive.

When the river flow is at the sea's mouth,

envy isn't so receptive.

It's ambivalent strange theory that's exceptive.

NEOLOGIC THOUGHT

Scuba diving in love's open heart can be wondrous and mysterious as The Great Barrier Reef-

There, the people are aquatic sea urchins, and their indistinct as heart ache is to grief-

and those transformations are never brief-

that's why it's not beyond the realm of belief.

40) Haphazard Love Affair's

'An inquisitive look from afar-

that's piqued her interest,

after having drank way too many at the bar-

has left the both of you with this impaired rational,

carelessly eliciting random night caps,

no matter how trite or bazar-

just as long as you two make it to his car-

for what's hoped to be an insatiable tryst of unadulterated sex,

sans the emotional scars-

but after this night of invigorating coitus,

you both awaken not knowing who each other are.

This is just one episodic tale from our questionable mating rituals-

these impromptu hook-ups,

have a way of morphing into exploitive and distortive look-ups that have become socially habitual-

This isn't only directed towards single individuals-

and the approximant numbers skew,

NEOLOGIC THOUGHT

the moral account of actual residuals

this type of misguided love reinterprets sexual companionships as being a relationship,

which becomes blinded and can't see the right signs that are visual.

41) An Abortive Affair

A toxic relationship has a way of potentially poisoning any future liaisons-

this can infect your new paramour with all your past bullshit,

until its leitmotif becomes too much for anyone to hang on-

and that's when hopes of starting anew are gone.

These fleeting moments of sexual aleatory-

can't compensate for the heart's longing for genuine effectual amatory-

When our amorous feelings give rise

we can't devise

enough lies

too disguise our behavior that's suddenly transitory-

and it should come as no surprise,

why it becomes the end to your sorted story.

42) Aristocratic Greed

An "esurience" for more

speaks to one's insatiable appetite-

for a wealthy privileged few,

it's viewed as a birth rite-

These parasites continue to amass fortunes at the expense of America's plebiscite-

with no end in sight-

Even the Vatican and the Scottish Rite-

could be contrite-

despite, having all this economic might.

Mankind's future continues to dim and doesn't seem as bright-

maybe the reason is the acceptance and quest to be America's new class of sybarites-

This may account for the lack in comprehensive financial over-sight.

This abnormal need to consume-

can lead to one's mortal doom-

especially, during times of great economic booms.

But, to these kind of people,

there's never enough liquidity to go around

Head-lines attest to the cupidity by C.E.O(s)

who've abscond-

with the pilfered fund's that abound,

cyphered thru complex networks below and above ground.

So, when it comes to stealing and scheming,

it accounts for only half the intrigue-

the lustful feeling of corruption at work compensates for any moral fatigue.

NEOLOGIC THOUGHT

43) Serpentine Minions

These "Buy"-partisan agents operate with complete impunity-

fore their plutocratic master's insure them of absolute immunity-

Unbeknownst to most of us,

we continue to cater to this lunacy-

It's coordinated sycophancy run amok,

an a-moralist plan of synergistic psycho-fancy.

When the line of demarcation has been drawn between the haves and the have not's-

thought patrolled intercessors furtively roll out belief and relief packets,

as if we're 18th century French peasants being cavorted by religiously fanatic Huguenots.

Religion and Capitalism has militated this postmodern

posterity obitum-

Claiming all life and future death was predetermine post-partum-

However, incessant paternalism has bequeath to an feign enlighten mankind,

offer this surrogate doctrine of belief that portends,

life is better lived postmortem.

44) Identity Sweep

In this age of instant and direct messages-

Amassed media's use of illusory antics,

has distorted most of the cognitive images.

The F.C.C.'s prevaricated assent with government lobbyist firms,

protect only those who give as loyal vassalages-

An unethical alignment that ensnares these

ex-afficials into pushing thru legislative bills and amendments,

that's assured of clear passages-

Whatever vestige of integrity they have left,

has become an auction-able commodity of advantage-

So say's corruptions' time held adage.

This accumulative effect-

is something the average person never suspects-

it's also how corporations protect-

those invasive marketing schemes,

because they accomplishes the desired affect-

which turns the unsuspecting citizen into

NEOLOGIC THOUGHT

consumptive automatons whether willing or without circumspect-

however implied or direct-

The planet's populace will forever be experimental subjects-

An esoteric agenda of corporate and government superintendents-

which continues an exorbitant pace towards economic profits-

and leaves the door further open for future prospects-

just as long as individualism is kept in check-

This Identity cleansing is truly perfected.

45) When Life Becomes Worth-Less

As mankind descends and evolution changes-

nature revalues the conscience in our brains-

we'll have no power to refrain-

from the dangerous inclinations the rationale entertains- at which point life starts to accept its disdain-

and suicidal thought's will make this type of behavior harder to explain-

especially, when this depression fuels your pain-

and any hope isn't easily ascertained

A toll taken from life's emotive drain-

because of the overwhelming pressure' your forced to mask the shame-

This type of mental hurt is never dull or plain-

social dysfunction is the price for pursuing ghetto fame- seriously, how vain!

Now look at the astronomical cost-

a once promising young life now lost.

NEOLOGIC THOUGHT

46) The Imperative to Know They-Self

There are depths within a person's despair

that epitomize the essence of an abyss-

where the pressures from an abhorrent mind

triggers most of its functions too desist-

these psychoactive disturbances

once activated starts to fight the conscious mind to exist.

How does one find themselves when they haven't a clue where to look-

the answer to this quandary isn't so puzzling

when your self-serving character convey you as this open book-

If introspection was all it took-

-metaphorically speaking-

You'd be off the muthafuckin' hook.

A true reversion to the conscientious self-

rids any stigmas that were placed on the Identities' moral wealth-

this synaptic transfer of your mental resources

can replenish the mind's mental health-with no psycho-tropic toxins needed

NEOLOGIC THOUGHT

as the emotive spirits convoy is moved by stealth-

While it's trying to reintegrate with the conscience in self.

47) Realistic Talk

A sentient life is serious no matter how we view it-

The reality of death is inevitable

so stop trying to pursue it.

These are two contravening certainties that are placed before man-

which hasn't allowed modern scientific anthropology

a chance to decipher the creative nature

in evolutions sublime plan.

As humans we continue to seek answers

to an enigma with no apparent end-

the paradox in this conundrum if ever solved

would virtually be impossible to apprehend.

So how or why did life begin?

we're still no closer to figuring out humanities origins-

even in thought

we rationalize, hypothesize, and even theorize the true meaning of sin-

and with so many varying degrees of mental seasoning, most people will exhibit disproportionate amounts

NEOLOGIC THOUGHT

of clear cerebral reasoning.

Logic is a proving equation-

however,

skepticism prohibits precise and concise thought actuation.

48) Mentally Entwined

I have these reoccurring visions

which plague my thoughts-

un-relinquishing the imagery my mind has fought-

over and over the mind was taught-

never to capitulate until conscious reasoning has been sought.

But, the chaotic scenery in my mind's eye

lacks lucid cohesion left is a scattered conscience

marred with myopic lesions.

This cognition that's been altered in station-

has opened the mind's door for neurotic infiltration-

Now the subconscious mind is tasked

with rationale interpretation-

and once pyrrhic episodes become a part of this equation-

any mental delusions can reinterpret the psyches adaptation-

In which, an otherwise normal person could abruptly

start to exhibit signs of mental deprecation-

"Damn, what an unpleasant realization.

49) The Shattered Essence

When the self is lost and hard to find-

it becomes paramount to reconnect

the self to its conscious mind.

Though the paradigm may differ from person to person

the essential aspects of the self

will not cede to mental usurpation.

People have allowed trivial pursuits to rule and

dictate their lives until it's ran them aground-

Forgetting civility and amenity

because these acts of social decorum no longer seems sound.

It's the what that controls our desires,

that have allowed reason and apprehension to abscond-

We're no longer bound by the virtues of brotherhood,

especially, in the inner-city neighborhoods,

Where there aren't any emotional gains

only real emotive pain and once spiritual healing has failed-

you know hope is on its way out as well.

50) Shape Shifter's

Legend has it,

"they thrive below the surface floor-

and for eons, have withstood severe climatic bore's-

these Neo-Amphibious entities hold the genetic key,

to unlocking "humanities enigmatic" door.

Scientific analysis reveals this shared R-Complex gene variant-

which is also inherent,

to the cerebral cortex's human helmet-

This piece of data highlights the blue prints to creations codex and humanity becomes transparent-

especially, since our origin's hint at an ancient single sex gamete-

but, modern science is led by a mysterious pretext and its not so apparent.

These "Terrestrial alien's" are somewhat like the furtive chameleon-

Whose body applicator adapts to nature's power source as does the vermillion-

NEOLOGIC THOUGHT

this is how these shape shifters mimic the forms of human's and then transform back into reptilian. This forging of two distinct species,

both are cold-blooded, one in nature,

the other its natural.

On television, their called: The Visitor's or '**V**'-

but in reality,

they look like you and me.

51) The Prism of Life

Try to imagine your life being viewed through the sphere of a multidimensional prism-

But, in this alternate reality,

time is construed as "enliven monism"-

and there isn't inter-dimensional parallelism.

In this paradoxical scheme-

Pandora's box is apart of the illogical theme-

an avatar's virtual virulence,

where reality is the dream-

far fetch you may scream-

but. the prism of life isn't always what it seems.

There are many conflicting aspects to life's elucidation-

it makes the ortality equation-

out too being an hypothesis intimation.

Although the conscious self and its soul speaks of a higher service-

The modern conscience in thought,

NEOLOGIC THOUGHT

deem we're interconnected sentients with a specific purpose.

In our ever-curious quest for greater illumination into our "paleontological" beginning's-

society continually reverts back to those lost ideas from an uncouth origin and our essence is confined for spiritual reasons.

52) Rimz' Timz' and Gemz

With the advent of the bling generation-

our young people have become mesmerized,

with materialized thing adulation.

Vehicle ware is sought after urban fare-

22 and 30 inch car rims have captured their glare-

with a misplaced valuation on life that's continued to captivate their delight just like a drum bass' snare.

Most shoes are made to protect the wearer's feet-

but not for these cream-colored boots',

that rule the foreign sands and rep the street[s]-

Not even hood staple's like Air Force Vs and Air Jordan's possess the durability to compete-

from the prison yard's,

to the War Zone theater's from afar,

these Gold hue shoes can't be beat-

and the Timberland company appreciates all the financial adoration that it reaps.

NEOLOGIC THOUGHT

And to those "shinny" objects that has dazzled their visual corneas'-

they wouldn't care if it's gold, platinum and diamonds,

hell, they'll even rock cubic zirconia's.

These fool's think (b.b.s) certified clear stones are the fairest-

truth is, bort-stones aren't pure or the rarest.

This lure of mineral ice,

has turned our youth into material megalomaniacs-

these slick diamond broker's,

who cop conflict stone from Africa's impoverished workers, which are later refined and then cartel'ed by 200 of the planet's preeminent Gemological brainiacs.

Purchased from a real or fake jeweler's cornucopia-

all in an attempt to be a part of some vain illusionary social utopia-

Open up those eye's"oh you can't" because you're now blinded from material myopia.

AH'KHEMU
a.k.a. Cebron Wade

Profile —

About the social poet / essayist —

Ah'khemu was born in Phoenix, Arizona on 5-24-74 and has lived in the greater bay area since the age of 5. His unique approach — through poetics — allows for the urban and suburban young adults, to fully recognize their 'MENTAL VALUE' in this neoteric age.

With this form of socialized edu-tainment. The hope is to enlighten and inspire an imagistic generation consumed with technologic fodder... that's becoming their demotic idiom.

These poems vary in style and substance for the sole purpose of multiple conveyance. Five unique categories are arranged to give the reader a broad perspective on urban literary intellect. From the street demographic to the intellectual leanings of academia, these poems evince the complex issues that face all of America's semi-

educated black youth. These poems are tailored to inform, refute, reclaim, reignite and redefine the black urban mind set.

The title it- self makes this type of poetry audacious, yet, compelling enough to consider its poetic value!
Ah'Khemu February '2017

Available Now...
@www.amazon.com

It's Hard Being The Same. By Eric Curtis

Roxxy' By A.C. Bellard

Ideas More Powerful Than Force. By Ricky Gaines II

Triumph. By Mesro

Coming Soon...

Street Karma. By Leo Fountila IV

Only A Chosen Few. By Mack Malik

* *

For ordering info please visit our website or call
www.capgainesllc.com –302-433-6777

CAPITAL GAINES LLC
4023 Kennett Pike #2082
Wilmington, Delaware 19807
www.capgainesllc.com
Telephone: (415-857-5433)
Email: cg@capgainesllc.com

MAIL PAYMENT TO:

CAPITAL GAINES LLC
4023 Kennett Pike #2082   ORDER YOUR BOOKS AND HAVE THEM DELIVERED QUICKLY
Wilmington, Delaware 19807

TITLE OF BOOK	QUANTITY EACH	TOTAL QUANTITY	METHOD OF PAYMENT	PRICE EACH	TOTAL PRICE
IDEAS MORE POWERFUL THAN FORCE				$15.00	
IT'S HARD BEING THE SAME				$15.00	
ROXXY				$15.00	
TRIUMPH				$10.00	
NEOLOGIC THOUGHT				$10.00	
STREET KARMA				$15.00	
ONLY A CHOOSEN FEW				$15.00	
TOTAL					

SHIP TO: FROM:

NAME:
ADDRESS:
CITY/STATE/ZIP CODE:
PHONE:
EMAIL:

NAME:
ADDRESS:
CITY/STATE/ZIP CODE: